Deserts

KINGFISHER

a Houghton Mifflin Company imprint
222 Berkeley Street
Boston, Massachusetts 02116
www.houghtonmifflinbooks.com

First published in 2005
2 4 6 8 10 9 7 5 3
2TR/0206/PROSP/RNB(RNB)/140MA/F

LIBRARY OF CONGRESS CATALOGING-IN-PUBLICATION DATA
Davies, Nicola, 1958-
Deserts/Nicola Davies.— 1st ed.
p. cm. — (Kingfisher young knowledge)
Includes index.
1. Deserts—Juvenile literature. I. Title. II. Series.
QH88.D38 2005
910'.02154—dc22   2004020233

ISBN 0-7534-5866-7
ISBN 978-07534-5866-2

Printed in China

Editor: Jennifer Schofield
Coordinating editor: Caitlin Doyle
Senior designer: Carol Ann Davis
Cover designer: Poppy Jenkins
Picture manager: Cee Weston-Baker
DTP manager: Nicky Studdart
DTP editor: Primrose Burton
Production controller: Jessamy Oldfield

Acknowledgments
The publishers would like to thank the following for permission to reproduce their material. Every care has been taken
to trace copyright holders. However, if there have been unintentional omissions or failure to trace copyright holders,
we apologize and will, if informed, endeavor to make corrections in any future edition.
b = bottom, c = center, l = left, t = top, r = right

Cover: Alamy/Lenscapp; page 1: Getty Imagebank; 2–3 Corbis/Firefly Productions; 4–5 Corbis/Gavriel Jecan; 6–7 Getty Taxi; 8t Panoramic
Images/Warren Marr; 8b Corbis/Dean Conger; 9t Corbis/Michael & Patricia Fogden; 9b Corbis/Owen Franken; 10–11 Still Pictures/
Frans Lemmens; 11t Corbis/Peter Johnson; 11b Corbis/Peter Johnson; 12–13 Corbis/Peter Lillie; Gallo Images; 12t Panoramic Images/
Warren Marr; 12b Science Photo Library/David Scharf; 14–15 Getty Taxi; 14b Getty Imagebank; 15tr Corbis/Dewitt Jones;
15br Corbis/Martin Harvey; Gallo Images; 16–17 Getty National Geographic; 16cr Getty Imagebank; 16b NHPA/Darryl Balfour;
17cl NHPA/Martin Harvey; 17r Corbis; 18–19 Ardea/John Cancalosi; 18 Ardea/Pat Morris; 19 Minden Pictures ; 20–21 Corbis; 20cl Minden
Pictures; 20b Frank Lane Picture Agency; 21tr Michael & Patricia Fogden; 21br NHPA/Daniel Heuclin; 22–23 Getty Imagebank;
22cr Corbis/Martin Harvey; Gallo Images; 23tr Ardea/Ken Lucas; 24–25 Getty Photographer's Choice; 25tr Corbis/Hans Georg Roth;
26–27 Still Pictures; 27tr Corbis/Richard Powers; 28–29 Still Pictures; 29tr Corbis/Derek Trask; 30–31 Still Pictures; 30b Corbis/Janet Jarman;
31tr Science Photo Library/Peter Ryan; 32–33 Corbis/KM Westermann; 32bl Getty Imagebank; 33br Getty Imagebank; 34–35 Getty Stone;
34cl Corbis; 35t Corbis/Carl & Ann Purcell; 35c Corbis/Paul A. Souders; 36–37 Corbis/Sergio Pitamitz; 36b Getty Stone; 37br Corbis/
Hughes Martin; 38–39 Science Photo Library/Martin Bond; 38b British Museum; 39t Getty National Geographic; 39b Corbis/James L. Amos;
40–41 Alamy/Steve Bloom; 41t Getty National Geographic; 48 Corbis/ Nigel J. Dennis; Gallo Images

Commissioned artwork on page 7 by Encompass Graphics
Commissioned photography on pages 42–47 by Andy Crawford. Project maker and photo shoot coordinator: Miranda Kennedy
Thank you to models Lewis Manu and Rebecca Roper.

Kingfisher Young Knowledge

Deserts

Nicola Davies

WITHDRAWN

KINGFISHER

Contents

What is a desert?

A desert is a place where it almost never rains. This makes these areas the driest places on Earth and the most difficult places to live in.

All around the world

One fourth of our planet is covered in deserts. Wherever there is a desert, there are animals and plants that have found a way to survive in the harsh and dry conditions.

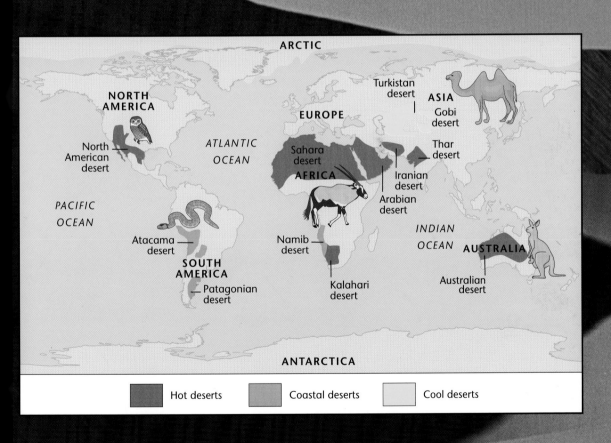

ARCTIC

NORTH AMERICA

EUROPE

Turkistan desert

ASIA

Gobi desert

North American desert

ATLANTIC OCEAN

Sahara desert

AFRICA

Thar desert

Iranian desert

Arabian desert

PACIFIC OCEAN

Atacama desert

SOUTH AMERICA

Namib desert

INDIAN OCEAN

AUSTRALIA

Kalahari desert

Australian desert

Patagonian desert

ANTARCTICA

| Hot deserts | Coastal deserts | Cool deserts |

conditions—how things are around you

Looking different

Not all deserts are hot and sandy. They can be pebbly, cool, rocky, mountainous, or even a mixture of all of these. Every desert is unique!

Hot Mojave

The Mojave desert in North America was once the bottom of a lake. Now it is a huge plain covered in cracked, dried mud and pebbles.

Cool Gobi

In Mongolia's Gobi desert the wind always blows in the same direction. This shapes the sand dunes and pushes them forward.

plain—a flat surface

Hot Sahara

These rocks are found in mountains that are part of the Sahara desert. They are so high that in the winter they are covered in frost.

Coastal desert

Fog blows in from the sea next to the Namib desert. This brings water to some of the highest sand dunes in the world.

fog—a low cloud made up of tiny drops of water

Wild weather

Desert weather is extreme. Clear blue skies mean that deserts are almost always sunny and hot during the day. But at night it is a very different story.

Chilly nights

With no clouds to hold in the day's heat, nights in the desert are very cold. Desert people light fires to stay warm after it gets dark.

extreme weather—very hot or very cold

Roasting days

It may be freezing at midnight, but by midday in the desert it is really hot. Animals, such as these springbok, have to shelter from the sun.

Staying warm . . . and cool

Desert squirrels, or ground squirrels, use their bushy tails to help them cope with extreme types of weather. During the cold night the squirrel's tail is like a fluffy blanket. But during the hot day it provides shade from the sun.

Whistling wind

Deserts are so windy that almost every one has a type of wind with its own special name. For example, the wind in Algeria is called the khamsin, and in North America it is called the chubaseos.

Dusty gusts!

Sometimes desert winds pick up sand and dust and blow them around in storms that can last for several days. This makes it difficult to see and even to breathe.

gusts—*sudden blasts of wind*

Sandy sculpture

Gusts full of sand and dust slowly wear away rocks.
Over thousands of years the rocks are transformed
into strange shapes such as these rocks found
in the Mojave desert.

Smoothest sand

Desert wind rubs the
sand grains together.
This makes the grains
smooth and round.

transformed—changed

Desert rain

Rain in the desert is very rare. So when there are showers, desert plants and animals have to make the most of them.

Stormy weather

Heavy rain often comes after thunder and lightning. In some deserts storms bring rain every year, but other deserts can stay dry for more than ten years.

rare—when something does not happen often

Be quick!

As soon as it rains, frogs lay their eggs in the pools of rainwater. Their tadpoles must grow quickly and change into frogs before the pools dry out.

Beautiful blooms

Desert plants flower after it rains, so the whole desert looks like a carpet of blossoms. When the flowers dry out and die, they leave seeds behind. These seeds sprout the next time it rains.

tadpoles—young frogs and toads

Prickly plants

Desert plants are tough. They have thicker skins, smaller leaves, and more spines than other plants. This stops the heat from drying them out and keeps hungry mouths away.

Drop that leaf!

Creosote bushes in North America drop their leaves when it is dry. But when it rains, they grow them again.

The Namib's dew collector

Leaves of the strange-looking welwitschia plant bend over onto the ground. Fog and dew stick to the leaves, making droplets of water that run down to the roots.

Lots of spikes

Saguaro cacti from Arizona have no leaves. Instead they store water in their huge stems. These stems are protected by thick skin and lots of prickly spikes.

Hide-and-seek!

Only the tops of the stone plant's two fat leaves poke out above the ground's surface. The plant hides from the sun and drying winds until it rains and is able to flower.

dew—*small drops of water that form during the night on grass and plants*

Desert fliers

Flight makes desert life easier for birds because they can travel long distances to find food and water. But they still have to cope with the hot days and cold nights.

Burrow nester

The tiny elf owl makes use of the cool twilight to hunt for small mammals, reptiles, and insects. It nests underground where its eggs are protected from the fierce heat that could cook them in their shells.

twilight—*when it is not dark or light, either at dawn or at dusk*

Cacti surgeons

Woodpeckers make holes in the rotten or broken stems of giant saguaro cacti. The woodpeckers nest in the cool holes and peck away at any sick parts of a cactus. This stops disease from spreading to the whole plant.

Roadrunner stretches

Desert roadrunners warm up after the cold desert night by lifting their neck feathers and letting the sun shine on a patch of special skin. This skin soaks up the heat and keeps them warm.

Little creatures

Insects, reptiles, and rodents thrive in the desert because they do not need much water. They can also hide from the heat, wind, or cold in burrows.

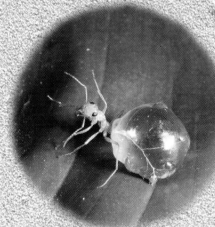

Honey bellies

Desert honey ants, or honeypot ants, store precious water and nectar in their inflated bellies. This supply helps the ant colony survive when there is no food or water.

Sleep at night

Reptiles, such as this chuckwalla, stay underground during the cold night. When morning comes, they lie in the sun to warm up.

burrows—holes or tunnels under the ground

og bathers

Darkling beetles find something to drink by tapping the droplets of water from fog on their legs and tipping them toward their mouths.

Sleep during the day

Animals like this little gerbil are warm-blooded. They search for food during the cold night, but in the daytime they need to hide underground in burrows to stay cool.

warm-blooded—body temperature that is always warm

Mighty mammals

Large mammals that live in deserts cannot find shelter from the sun in burrows like their smaller relatives. So they must find other ways to beat the heat.

Dig out to chill out
To cool off their bellies, kangaroos scrape away at the hot surface sand and lie down on the colder sand underneath.

mammals—warm-blooded animals that feed their young on mother's milk

Color coded

Fennec foxes' pale fur helps reflect the heat and keep them cool—just like a white T-shirt will keep you cool on a hot summer's day.

Camel cooler

At night camels' bodies become really cold. So although the sun warms them all day long, they are never too hot.

reflect—to send back or aside

Pools of water

Rivers flowing through the desert or bubbling up from under the ground can bring water all year-round to deserts. A place where this happens is called an oasis.

Green and growing

Oases are bustling with life. Tall trees, such as palms, and many types of animals can live in oases because there is plenty of water.

bustling—busy

Walking to water

Oases are very important to desert people and their animals. They may travel hundreds of miles to find water at a familiar oasis— even if the water is at the bottom of a well.

well—*a deep hole in the ground with water at the bottom*

Desert dwellers

People have lived in deserts for thousands of years. They have learned all types of ways to cope with the difficulties of desert life.

People who wander
Many desert people are nomads. They live in tents and move around to find freshwater and grazing for their animals.

nomads—*people who move from place to place, taking their homes with them*

Water carriers

Women in India's Thar desert carry water from faraway wells in large jars that they balance on their heads.

Growing deserts

Deserts are beautiful and important wild places. But they are expanding unnaturally because of some of the things that humans do. Every year deserts swallow up valuable grasslands, farmlands, and forests.

Too much munching

Where people let their animals eat all the plants, the sun and wind can hit the bare ground. This turns the soil into dust and makes it difficult to regrow plants.

expanding—getting bigger

Bad gas!

Cars, airplanes, and factories emit gases that make the weather hotter. This is called global warming. It is worse in places that are already hot and dry, so it makes deserts grow.

emit—to give off

Making deserts green

People can help stop deserts from expanding by planting trees and grass to protect the soil. Irrigating the desert helps keep the plants alive.

Rain saving

Saving rainwater with dams means that there will be water for crops. This woman is harvesting food in what was once desert.

irrigating—watering big areas such as whole fields

Magic water

Usually water runs through sand and is lost. Adding flakes of special plastic to the water helps soil hold onto it and allows plants to grow.

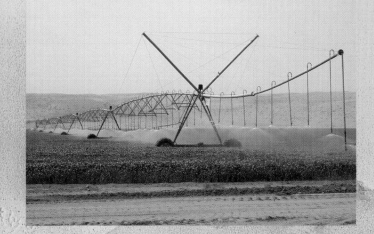

Green . . . and greener

Growing plants also helps cool the ground and the air above. This means that the soil stays moist and the desert cannot expand.

moist—damp

Cities in the desert

There are cities in deserts all over the world. But cities with millions of people use a lot of water—and that is a big problem in any desert!

Bright lights, big city

Las Vegas, in the Nevada desert, is so big that it uses water from hundreds of miles away. This lack of water threatens both the wildlife and farmland with droughts.

drought—a long period of time when there is no water

Green, green city

Abu Dhabi, on the coast of the
United Arab Emirates, uses freshwater
from the sea by taking out the salt.
This means that there is enough
water to create green spaces
that keep the city cool.

Ways to save water

Kerzaz, an ancient city in
the Sahara desert, needs
much less water than a
modern town.
People there
use water
carefully and
know that
every drop is
very precious.

Using the desert

Deserts may look empty, but they have hidden treasures. They also give us the space to do things that are dangerous anywhere else.

Deadly testing

The world's deadliest weapons, nuclear bombs, are tested in deserts where they cannot kill anyone. But these bombs leave the land poisoned for many years after testing.

Hidden energy

Petroleum is found under some deserts. It is pumped and carried to cities and other countries in huge pipes like this one.

Underground jewels

Opals were formed millions of years ago when water drained from rocks under the ground. This ground is now the Australian desert, and almost all of the world's opals are mined there!

petroleum—the oil used to make fuel for cars, electricity, and many plastics

Lots of fun!

Sunny, blue skies and beautiful scenery make deserts great places to relax, but some people like a little more action.

Sand boarding

You can go down a sand dune in exactly the same way as you would slide down a snowy slope. You can even surf a dune like a big wave in the sea!

Desert racer

Dune buggies can climb steep dunes and zoom around the desert without getting stuck in the sand. They are a lot of fun, but their tires can damage desert plants.

Comfortable climbing

Rock formations found in deserts are warm and dry. This makes them easier to climb than mountains, where the weather can be cold, wet, and icy.

History in the desert

We can learn about the past in deserts because the hot, dry air preserves dead bodies. Sand covers the dried remains of people, plants, and animals, and because few people live in deserts, they can lie undisturbed for a long time.

Mummies from long ago

Bodies buried in deserts dry out very quickly, so skin, hair, and clothes can last for thousands of years. Preserved dead bodies, called mummies, found in deserts show us how people looked and dressed a long time ago.

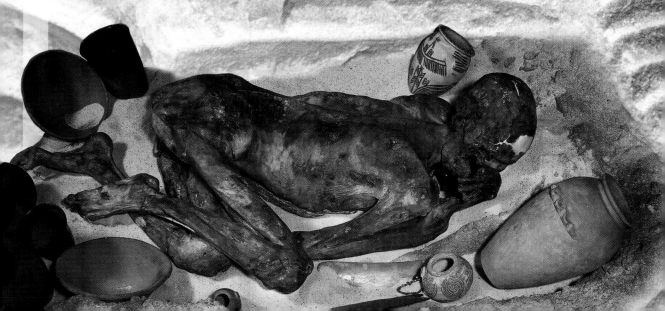

Rock art

Thousands
of years ago
people painted
pictures on rocks in the
Namib desert. The pictures show that
the desert used to be grassland
bustling with people and animals.

Desert dinos

Some of the world's most
exciting dinosaur fossils
have been found in deserts.
The dry winds wear away
the rocks and bring fossil
bones close to the surface.

fossils—the remains of ancient animals or plants turned to rock

Ice and water

Not all deserts are hot and dusty—some are not even dry! The word "desert" can also be used to describe places where conditions are simply too tough for life to survive.

Lifeless blue

There can be no life in the sea without phytoplankton. In places where plankton does not grow the sea can be a wet and salty desert.

Icy deserts

Some parts of the Arctic get less rain than Africa's Sahara desert. These areas are too cold and dry for anything to grow. Polar bears survive by walking to the sea to catch seals.

phytoplankton—tiny floating plants found in oceans and seas

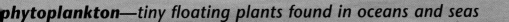

Crazy camels

Salt train

Selling salt is a very important way for desert people to make money. Loads of salt are carried across the desert on camels.

camel template

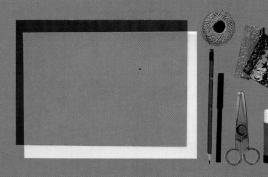

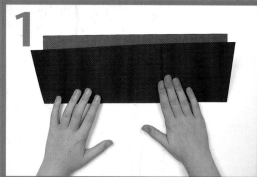

1 Fold the brown cardboard in half. Put the piece of tracing paper over the camel template and trace around the camel shape.

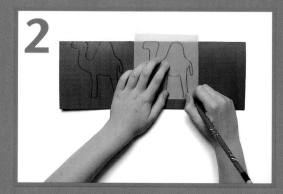

2 Put the traced template onto the cardboard so that the camel's hump is on the fold. Trace the camel onto the cardboard to make three camels.

3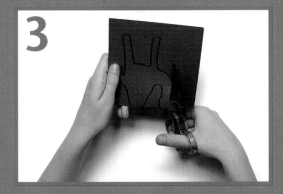

Using the scissors, carefully cut out the three camel shapes. Make sure that you do not cut through the humps along the fold.

4

Holding the camel down firmly with one hand, use the permanent marker to draw the eyes and mouth on both sides of each camel.

5

Smooth out three different foil candy bar wrappers. Paste them over the middle of the camels' backs. You may need to cut the wrappers if they are too long.

6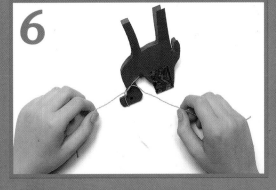

To make the camels' bridles, tie thread around the camels' necks. Use the thread to join the camels together so that they are ready to carry salt across the desert.

3-D cactus

Slit and slide!

The saguaro cactus can be more than 30 feet tall and can have five arms. Some saguaro are more than 200 years old!

You will need
- Pencil
- Scissors
- Tracing paper
- Thick green cardboard

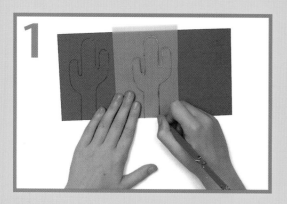

1

Trace the cactus template onto the tracing paper. Then use the template to trace two cacti onto the green cardboard.

2

Cut out the two cactus shapes. Following the template, use the scissors from the top to cut a slit halfway down one cactus.

slit 1 (step 2)

cactus template

slit 2 (step 3)

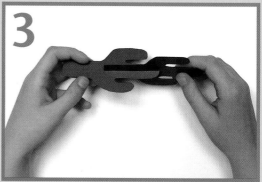

3

From the bottom cut a slit halfway up the second cactus. Slide the first cactus into the second. If you want to, you can decorate the cactus with green glitter.

Palm trees

Bend and shape it!

Palm trees are often found at oases in the Sahara. Desert people rest in the shade of the palms when it is hot.

You will need
- 2 strips of brown cardboard
- Glue
- Green cardboard
- Double-sided tape
- Shoe box lid
- Sand

1

To make the palm tree's trunk, glue the brown cardboard to make an "L" shape. Fold the cardboard over itself to make an accordion tube.

2

To make the palm tree's leaves, cut the green cardboard into five curved strips. Fold each strip like a fan, and it will spring open.

Fill a shoe box lid with sand and put the camels, 3-D cactus, and palm tree in the tray to create your own desert landscape.

3

Cut a small piece of double-sided tape and stick it in the middle of the palm tree's trunk. Stick each of the five leaves onto the trunk.

Aboriginal spinning top

Clever symbols

The aborigines of Australia's desert painted symbols on rocks. Now artists use these symbols to paint modern art.

You will need

- Pencil
- Mug
- Cup
- Small plate
- Cardboard
- Scissors
- Paint
- Paintbrush
- Modeling clay
- Compass
- Chopstick

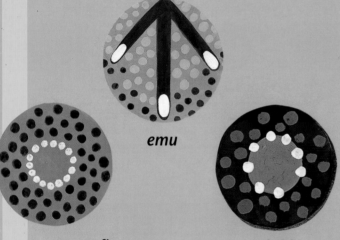

emu

campfire

child

1

To make five disks, trace on the cardboard around a mug two times, a cup two times, and a small plate once. Carefully cut out each disk.

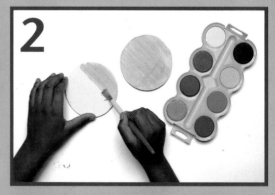

2

Paint the disks using orange or yellow paint—if you want, each circle can be a different color. Leave the disks to dry completely.

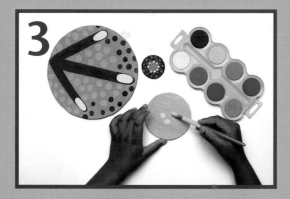

3 Following the examples on page 46, paint one side of each disk with a different aboriginal symbol. When the paint is dry, turn the disks over and paint the same symbol on the other side.

4 Put a ball of modeling clay under the middle of each disk. Use the point of the compass to pierce a hole in the middle of each disk.

When all five disks are on the chopstick, stand the top upright and spin it around.

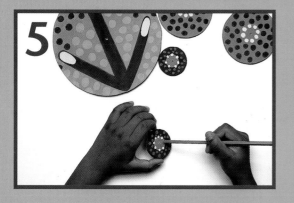

5 To put the disks on the chopstick, start with one of the disks from the cup and the mug and then the disk from the plate and the last two from the mug and cup. The disks should be spaced evenly.

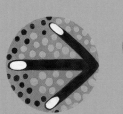

Index